Inexplicable Joy

Inexplicable Joy

On the Heart Sutra

Susan Piver

© Susan Piver 2025

All rights reserved. No part of this book may be reproduced, stored in a retrieval system, or transmitted, in any form or by any means, without the prior written consent of the publisher, except in the case of brief quotations embodied in reviews and articles.

Lionheart Press, Somerville, MA, USA
lionheartpress.net

Library of Congress Control Number: 2024950055
ISBN 978-1-7369439-3-9 (paperback)
ISBN 978-1-7369439-4-6 (e-book)

Also available in audiobook.

Cover & text design by Jazmin Welch (fleck creative studio)

For Sam

ABOUT THE SUTRA TRANSLATION: Lotsawa bhikuhu Rinchen De translated *The Sutra of the Heart of Transcendent Knowledge* into Tibetan with the Indian pandita Vimalamitra. It was edited by the great editor-lotsåwas Gelo, Namkha, and others. This Tibetan text was copied from the fresco in Gegye Chemaling at the glorious Samye vihara. It has been translated into English by the Nalanda Translation Committee under the direction of Vidyadhara the Venerable Chogyam Trungpa Rinpoche, with reference to several Sanskrit editions. © 1975, 1980 by the Nalanda Translation Committee. All rights reserved.

Contents

- 1   **INTRODUCTION**
- 9   **ENTERING THE CONVERSATION**
- 15   **IT'S A SPIRITUAL PRACTICE**
  - 16   THREE SACRED ACTS
  - 16   *Make Offerings*
  - 17   *Request Blessings*
  - 21   *Dedicate the Merit*
- 24   **THE SUTRA OF THE HEART OF TRANSCENDENT KNOWLEDGE**
- 29   **LINE-BY-LINE**
- 57   **ON CHANTING**
- 63   **IN CONCLUSION**
- 67   **RESOURCES**
- 68   **ACKNOWLEDGEMENTS**

INTRODUCTION

Profound and insightful books have been written about the *Prajnaparamita Sutra*, also known as *The Sutra of the Heart of Transcendent Knowledge*, or just the Heart Sutra. This is not one of them. Rather, it is an invitation to walk through the text with me, to be inspired, confused, frustrated, and delighted by it.

The Heart Sutra confounds. It would be easy to read it and think *this is crazy, what the hell?*, or *I will never understand this*, or most wrongheaded of all, *I think I get it*. In any case, whether by impatience or arrogance, a chasm would open up between you and it.

The words themselves are both ordinary (*Thus have I heard*) and extraordinary (*form is emptiness, emptiness also is form*). One could walk away from it and consider it as an ancient text that once had meaning in a long-gone cultural context or as an unfathomable, unfunny riddle requiring great spiritual erudition to comprehend.

For all its seeming opacity, the Heart Sutra remains a central text throughout the Buddhist world, particularly in Mahayana schools of thought, including the Zen tradition. It dates back to…some date. No one can really agree. 661 BCE? 100 BCE? 700 CE? It's not completely clear. We could also consider that it has always existed, authorless, hidden to be discovered by future beings like you and me through luck, timing, or various mishaps.

In accordance with the multi-layered and impenetrable nature of the Heart Sutra, it exists in a variety of editions. The longest version is rumored to be 100,000 lines long and comprise many volumes. Another version is slightly less intimidating at only 8,000 lines long. The version I recite and discuss in this work is 43 lines long. The ultimate version is zero lines long and only one syllable: AH. It's up to you which version you'd like to study.

Right now countless beings are reciting the Heart Sutra, no matter when "right now" is for you. If we could somehow hear all the voices chanting it in this moment, perhaps the beautiful, atonal cacophony would break through all our mental delusions. Add to that all the voices who have chanted it in the past and may in the future and the entire world might awaken from its suffering. May it be so.

Musings aside, though you are reading a small work written by me, I should mention that I do not understand the Heart Sutra at all. While I have been chanting it for more than three decades, I can't say I know more than I did the first time I chanted it in 1993. I encountered it when a great meditation teacher volunteered to teach me how to meditate. I had no idea why he was willing to do this, what to expect, or even much about him—we had only met once, at a party. Something inside me said DO IT, but I was still plenty nervous. Back then, meditation was still considered strange, and as mentioned, I didn't really know him. When I went over to his house, he kindly welcomed me and asked a few questions about my interest in meditation. I have no idea what I said in response. Then we sat on cushions on the floor opposite his very beautiful shrine, and he handed me a piece of paper with words printed on both sides. "We'll chant this together before we begin. It's called the Heart Sutra. Just follow along with me and skip over the words you can't pronounce."

It began:

> Thus have I heard. Once the Blessed One was dwelling in Rajagriha at Vulture Peak Mountain, together with a great gathering of the sangha of monks and a great gathering of the sangha of bodhisattvas. At that time the Blessed One entered the samadhi that expresses the dharma called "profound illumination"…

What did these words mean and why were we saying them? Sangha, bodhisattvas, samadhi? I had no idea, but I stumbled along as suggested. Then he taught me how to meditate and we sat together. He is still my meditation teacher.

Since that day, I have chanted the Heart Sutra countless times, nearly every day. I learned what all the words meant. I have gone on retreats focused on this text and nothing else. I memorized it long ago and if you woke me tonight from a sound sleep and asked me to recite the entire thing, I absolutely could.

Though I have not gained more in the way of understanding, my relationship to the text continues to deepen in ways that cannot be deconstructed, only observed. Each time I recite it, I find something I hadn't noticed before or had simply forgotten about. On good days, certain words jump out at me and provoke a flash of insight: *Oh, that must be what it means*. And then it disappears. In other words, there's a continuing dialogue between me and the Heart Sutra. Should you chant it, you will enter your own dialogue. What you will discuss together, I have no way of knowing.

Relating to the Heart Sutra is a little bit like falling in love. At first, there is swooning and marveling. Over time, if we are lucky, the original connection morphs into something both less exciting and more meaningful: true intimacy. Then, just like in actual human relationships, as such intimacy deepens it becomes clear that you will never really know each other. This intimate not-knowing seems to be the hallmark of the spiritual journey.

For me, nowhere is this juxtaposition more apparent (and satisfying, confounding, surprising, disappointing, comforting—just like a real relationship) than with the Heart Sutra. I hope it will be the same for you. I urge you to stay with it.

ENTERING THE CONVERSATION

Our mind tunes to a different channel when it encounters the Heart Sutra. Rather than picking up a station that broadcasts news 24-7 about how effed up you are, this channel speaks a non-retainable language. You understand what is being said the moment you hear it, and then it self-erases. I have no idea why. Because it is inscrutable and beyond conventional comprehension, it resists solidification into concept. It points over and over to the wisdom beyond conventional mind that seems to always reside 45 degrees away from you. You see it out of the corner of your eye, but each time you turn to look at it, it moves another 45 degrees. And another.

The sutra reveals itself through relationship rather than two-dimensional study. It kind of wants to make out with you.

Perhaps because of its emphasis on the emptiness that gives rise to all phenomena, it may not surprise you to hear that *Prajnaparamita* is also the name of a female deity. *Prajna* means wisdom and *paramita* means perfected. She is said to be the mother of all Buddhas, meaning, perhaps, that all awakened beings (*Buddha* means awake) are born of wisdom that is pure and absolute.

It is altogether reasonable to wonder what deities are doing in Buddhism at all. After all, it is a non-theistic tradition, one that posits neither a single god nor a pantheon of gods. One of its most surprising characteristics—and a factor that makes it possible for anyone to engage with its wisdom, no matter their belief system—is the absence of an external entity of any kind. There is no creator, no judge, no jury, no beneficent or maleficent figures lying in wait—nothing (and I do mean *nothing*) besides your own mind, which is inseparable from "mind-ness" itself.

This is an extremely difficult notion to grasp. Among the biggest mistakes one could make would be to "believe" it. All beliefs are dependently arisen, based on past experiences, others' opinions, books read, genetic structures, dreamscapes explored, songs, movies, physical health, and so on. Take away one missed connection, and the whole thing might fall apart.

Such beliefs may be deeply felt, poetic, incisive, nuanced, mappable. You may be able to provide many charts and graphs. You may even draw a belief that the Heart Sutra is "correct" (or "incorrect" for that matter). In Buddhist thought, all beliefs are considered obstacles because they separate you from what is now. And now. "Now," as the great Texas singer-songwriter Butch Hancock sings, "it's now again."

Within Buddhist practice, deities are not thought of as beings outside of ourselves keeping score, but as emanations of your own wisdom mind. When you look at a deity, be it the fierce and beautiful Prajnaparamita, the wrathful, befanged four-armed Mahakala, or even the Buddha himself, you are looking at yourself. When they look at you, presumably, they see themselves. There is no division because there is nothing separate from anything else. Only oneness that is both empty and utterly full. Prajnaparamita herself is an example of the fullness of this "nothing." We could consider it a great kindness when wisdom is transmogrified into human form because it gives us a chance to relate to it. The deities, female and male, wrathful and peaceful, present the opportunity to see ourselves in a different way.

Where to go with the idea that everything falls apart when believed in? Though I cannot answer this question, I have no doubt that Prajnaparamita can. The more we are confounded by her, the closer we come to the answer.

The word "heart" may indicate that the text is about emotions, but it refers to the pith, the essence. The 100,000 or 8,000 lines have been pared down to something a little more bite-sized. Please note that, like space food, each bite is packed with nutrients. One little bitty bite could contain a 108-course meal. You don't want to overdo it, so please take your time exploring this text.

As we begin our line-by-line exploration of *The Sutra of the Heart of Transcendent Knowledge*, I encourage you not to ask *what does this mean?* Instead ask *what does this mean to me?* Intimacy is predicated on just such a personal approach and Lady Prajnaparamita seems to respond more readily to the warmth of the inner world than anything academic.

IT'S A SPIRITUAL PRACTICE

As you may already know, mindfulness has taken hold in Western culture. It lives up to its reputation as a way to de-stress, pacify difficult emotions, and become more laser focused on the tasks at hand. I mean, science has proven it so. However, at some point, and this is based on decades of practice and observation of fellow practitioners (not to mention, myself), meditation will become boring and hard. Yes, that is the case, and I regret to inform you that anyone who says otherwise may not be lying, but it is also doubtful they are meditating.

As it turns out, some sense of boredom and uncertainty about the benefits of meditation are good signs. When we become bored, it may mean we have exhausted efforts to entertain ourselves by meditating. (*This is going to make me more awesome! I think I just experienced the ultimate truth! Everyone should meditate, how can I convince them to do so!*) Uncertainty about the direction the practice is taking creates a kind of mental fuzz that may enable us to see beyond what we are so sure about to begin with.

Think of boredom and uncertainty as twin noren curtains that divide the mundane and sacred realms for purposes of protection.

THREE SACRED ACTS

It is helpful to consider that mindfulness is not just a self-improvement tactic but a gateway to seeing beyond all such improvements. Maneuvering through this potentially lengthy phase of simply not knowing what is going on in meditation practice takes some tenacity. You might think *this isn't working*. Understandable. After all, we're trained from a very early age to be productive, look for results, and focus on success.

As it turns out, meditation is extraordinarily productive and consequential. It confers strange successes only recognizable in hindsight. We are simply unaccustomed to following a path that is non-linear and extremely personal. Spiritual insights exist beyond the hamster wheel of societally condoned self-help and the shaming and self-aggression that often accompany it. How to let go of this self-helpy context for practice and replant it in richer soil? Three steps can help protect the sacred nature of meditation.

Make Offerings

When you walk into a shrine room of any religion, there are often flowers, candles, and incense. These are offerings. You can make a similar type of setup in your home by creating a smaller version of a traditional shrine. Shrine objects tend to center around the senses: things you can see, smell, taste, touch, or hear. Images of respected figures, flowers or scented candles, sweets, beautiful fabrics, and music are often included in sacred spaces. A shrine or altar is a way of focusing the energy of these offerings, so a table covered in brocade holding a candle and a photograph is a very simple way of showcasing your offerings. Or you can simply place some fresh flowers next to a picture of someone or something you love and aspire to emulate. You can light a candle as an offering of warmth, light, and safety. It's not important to make your altar table the most beautiful in the history of the world. What is important is that it be clean and heartfelt.

And, when in doubt, the best offering is one you can always make, no matter where you are or how you feel and that is your own experience in the moment.

So, before meditation, touch in with how it feels to be you right now. Maybe you feel great, crappy, or all of the above.

Feel it. Offer it to whom or whatever you hold sacred by saying something like, "I offer exactly who I am right now to the highest wisdom and goodness I can imagine." You don't have to know exactly what this means, just rouse a sense of generosity.

Request Blessings

Requesting blessings requires you to give up knowing what a blessing looks like exactly. Requesting of the gods what you think will make you happy (*bring me my dream job*) is like making a reservation at a five-star restaurant and then asking if you can go back into the kitchen and cook your own meal.

Instead of cooking your own food, just try to order what sounds good. *Please let me feel satisfied in my work* is better than *please make me VP of Finance*. Other options include: *Please let me find love. I wish to be free of this pain. May my life be an act of service to this world. Show me the ultimate wisdom.* These are good, basic requests that will allow a master chef to serve you something that exceeds all expectations.

Requesting blessings is predicated on the assumption that greater powers are at work. This could mean any number of things to each of us. That greater power could be God, a deity, an angel, or the quality of human goodness. It could also be something unnameable and perhaps this is the most trustworthy power of all. It doesn't really matter what you call this greater power. The only thing that seems required is to not quite understand what it is. Whenever anyone seems to know with too much certainty just what this power is, where it lives, what it thinks, and the primary means of access, I become a bit suspicious. Sure, all sorts of explanations make sense. But the only thing I know is that the moment I think I understand the sacred oneness of existence, I've stepped outside of that oneness and therefore can't be trusted.

There is power in asking the greatest sources of wisdom you can imagine to bless you. Who do you ask? If you are a Christian, you could ask Jesus. If you are Buddhist, you can ask for your teacher's blessing or the blessings of the phenomenal world. You can seek the blessings of magic if you are an alchemist, Gandhi if you're a pacifist, the earth if you're a Pagan. The idea is to seek the blessings of *your* lineage. Your ancestors. Please be as creative as possible.

When I notice who I think of and wish for when I'm confused or troubled, I imagine my beloved teachers—Tulku Thondup Rinpoche, Sam Bercholz, Chogyam Trungpa, the Bodhisattva Manjusri, and Padmasambhava and Yeshe Tsogyal. The first two, I've had the excellent good fortune to meet and study with in person, to ask my questions, feel foolish, and always leave inspired. The others, I never met in person but I encounter in my mindstream constantly. (They speak to me in my own voice.)

There are other, non-Buddhist beings I notice myself thinking of and wishing I could speak to or walk with. Some are figures I respect and love due to their creations: the poet Rilke, the hermeticist Catherine MacCoun, and the deity known as John Coltrane. (For me, WWJCD means "What would John Coltrane do?") These are examples of figures who, to me (and many others), have cut through delusion with a double-edged sword to reveal a much bigger space than we could otherwise imagine.

Just sitting here typing these words, thinking of them, my eyes fill with tears. How did I get so lucky to have such companions? My heart is weighted with a painful gratitude. I will never be worthy. It's just a fact.

On the other hand…one of my greatest teachers, another person I never met, was named Uvaldo Luna. More than 30 years ago, he crashed into my car and threw me out the passenger door, out of my body, out of normalcy. No one expected me to live and to this day, I feel echoes of the many injuries. I have no idea what his experience was; we never exchanged two words. I'm not grateful to him, neither hate nor forgive him. But the course of my life was irrevocably altered by him, and so he is here with me, every minute of every day. It would do no good to ignore him.

Finally, I think of my own actual blood. Though I also never met them, 100 percent of my ancestors came from the same place: Ashkenazi Jewish parts of Ukraine and Russia. As with many of my generation, I grew up knowing nothing about them; my parents' fervent wish was to simply be American and avoid drawing too much attention to themselves. Attention leads to very bad things. I wish I knew anything about these ancestors, but in some ways I know everything about them because I see and feel who I am.

When I sit down to practice, I think of my Buddhist teachers, first, always, deeply. Through various chants I've been taught (including the Heart Sutra), I simply name check them. And though I don't say their names in the same way, I feel my ancestors by my side—Buddhist teachers to my right, ancestors to my left, a line of scrimmage, everyone angling toward a single, continuously moving goal.

What lineage do you belong to? Is it a religious tradition? Maybe so, maybe not. Maybe you're of the lineage of poets or scientists, of painters, mothers, CEOs, crusaders, or lovers. Think of those you've learned the most from, the voices you'd like to hear when you get confused, those you admire the most, so much that you feel embarrassed to even think you might be connected to them—a sure sign that they are your best heart-friends. Get a sense of your heart's lineage and, in whatever way feels natural to you, request the blessings of that line. You could say their names before you practice. You could write a little note to one or all. You could simply feel them pulsing within you and around you.

When you request blessings, no matter how certain you are of where and who they come from, allow a little bit of not knowing. Chanting the Heart Sutra is a perfect example of requesting blessings while not knowing anything.

Dedicate the Merit

Once you have finished your spiritual practice, connect with whatever benefit or confusion you may have created for yourself during this particular practice. Once you have this felt-sense, give it away. In whatever way feels natural for you, rouse the aspiration that the results of your practice could benefit all beings. (Remember: "all beings" includes you.)

Please read through *The Sutra of the Heart of Transcendent Knowledge*. As you do, let your mind wander. Think of the text not as a doctrine, but as a waking dream. Then we will look at it together, line by line.

THE SUTRA *of* THE HEART *of* TRANSCENDENT KNOWLEDGE

Thus have I heard. Once the Blessed One was dwelling in Rajagriha at Vulture Peak mountain, together with a great gathering of the sangha of monks and a great gathering of the sangha of bodhisattvas. At that time the Blessed One entered the samadhi that expresses the dharma called "profound illumination," and at the same time noble Avalokiteshvara, the bodhisattva mahasattva, while practicing the profound prajnaparamita, saw in this way: he saw the five skandhas to be empty of nature.

Then, through the power of the Buddha, venerable Shariputra said to noble Avalokiteshvara, the bodhisattva mahasattva, "How should a son or daughter of noble family train, who wishes to practice the profound prajnaparamita?"

Addressed in this way, noble Avalokiteshvara, the bodhisattva mahasattva, said to venerable Shariputra, "O Shariputra, a son or daughter of noble family who wishes to practice the profound prajnaparamita should see in this way: seeing the five skandhas to be empty of nature. Form is emptiness; emptiness also is form. Emptiness is no other than form; form is no other than emptiness. In the same way, feeling, perception, formation, and consciousness are emptiness. Thus, Shariputra, all dharmas are emptiness. There are no characteristics. There is no birth and no cessation. There is no impurity and no purity. There is no decrease and no increase. Therefore, Shariputra, in emptiness, there is no form, no feeling, no perception, no formation, no consciousness; no eye, no ear, no nose, no tongue, no body, no mind; no appearance, no sound, no smell, no taste, no touch, no dharmas; no eye dhatu up to no mind dhatu, no dhatu of dharmas, no mind consciousness dhatu;

no ignorance, no end of ignorance up to no old age and death, no end of old age and death; no suffering, no origin of suffering, no cessation of suffering, no path, no wisdom, no attainment, and no nonattainment. Therefore, Shariputra, since the bodhisattvas have no attainment, they abide by means of prajnaparamita. Since there is no obscuration of mind, there is no fear. They transcend falsity and attain complete nirvana. All the buddhas of the three times, by means of prajnaparamita, fully awaken to unsurpassable, true, complete enlightenment. Therefore, the great mantra of prajnaparamita, the mantra of great insight, the unsurpassed mantra, the unequaled mantra, the mantra that calms all suffering, should be known as truth, since there is no deception. The prajnaparamita mantra is said in this way:

OM GATE GATE PARAGATE PARASAMGATE BODHI SVAHA

Thus, Shariputra, the bodhisattva mahasattva should train in the profound prajnaparamita."

Then the Blessed One arose from that samadhi and praised noble Avalokiteshvara, the bodhisattva mahasattva, saying, "Good, good, O son of noble family; thus it is, O son of noble family, thus it is. One should practice the profound prajnaparamita just as you have taught and all the tathagatas will rejoice."

When the Blessed One had said this, venerable Shariputra and noble Avalokiteshvara, the bodhisattva mahasattva, that whole assembly and the world with its gods, humans, asuras, and gandharvas rejoiced and praised the words of the Blessed One.

LINE-BY-LINE

Thus have I heard.

The sutra is introduced by someone saying, *I was there and this is what I heard*, which implies, perhaps, that you may hear something different. In this case, the person doing the hearing was Ananda, one of the historic Buddha's primary attendants and his cousin. Ananda was known for his stellar memory and often acted as the Buddha's secretary. The Buddha riffed, and Ananda recorded it. So when he said "Thus have I heard," you can trust that it is accurate.

However, there is also room for you to be the one doing all the hearing. Who knows, maybe Ananda had a cold or something that day and missed this nuance or that. It behooves you to note what *you* hear. In this way, you are Ananda every single time you recite these words, or at least you could pretend you are. It is useful to approach the Heart Sutra by taking the seat of "I" right from the beginning, to make each listen fresh and personal, as if you never heard it before. And, trust me, you haven't. *What do I hear* is an important question to begin with. There are some works that can only ever be heard (or read) for the first time. This is one of them. Each time you will hear something different.

> Once the blessed one was dwelling in Rajagriha at Vulture Peak Mountain together with a great gathering of the sangha of monks and a great gathering of the sangha of bodhisattvas.

"Blessed one" refers to the Buddha, Siddhartha Guatama. Rajagriha was an important capital city in India during his lifetime. It is currently known as Rajgir (sometimes translated as "royal mountain") in the Nalanda District and remains a Buddhist pilgrimage site.

Ananda then noted that present were monks and bodhisattvas, equally. This gathering was not for one or the other exclusively. What is a bodhisattva and what is the difference between monks and bodhisattvas?

You could say that monks and bodhisattvas represent particular journeys to liberation. As I was taught, there are three main cycles of Buddhist teachings. The first cycle, sometimes called the Hinayana teachings, contains what is needed to enter the path to begin with. *Hina* means foundational and *yana* means vehicle. (Note: sometimes *hina* is translated as "lesser" but that leads to the mistaken idea that these teachings are inferior. They are most certainly not. Without them, we stumble around as if we tied our shoes together and then tried to walk. So I prefer foundational.) This vehicle presents the Four Noble Truths, an examination of the Middle Way, and the first version of the *Vinaya*, or code of ethics for monks and nuns. So "a great gathering of the sangha of monks" invokes the presence of the

Hinayana teachings with their emphasis on simplicity, discipline, and renunciation—qualities that are needed to embark on the spiritual journey. Liberation then comes after many lifetimes of purification and personal growth.

The next cycle of teachings from the Buddha, the Mahayana, focus on what we may be capable of or drawn to once a firm foothold in the Hinayana has been established. When we have some degree of stability in our personal practice, our hearts simply open to others. Organically. Naturally. Our wiring dictates it. *Maha* means greater, but this does not mean "better." Rather, the Mahayana teachings open us to the greater world and ask us to consider all who reside in it. They help us work with the fullness of heart that continually increases whether or not we would like it to. Here, the practitioners who commit to the path of love in both its forms—relative and absolute—are known as bodhisattvas. The journey to liberation is undertaken in order to help all beings to be liberated.

(Note: Though the Heart Sutra is deeply consonant with the teachings of the third cycle, the Vajrayana or "indestructible vehicle," these teachings had not yet been transmitted. Perhaps that is why no lineage figures are mentioned in the sutra.)

A great gathering of monks and bodhisattvas is like *the gang's all here*. The teaching to follow will benefit both Hinayana and Mahayana practitioners. No problem.

> At that time, the Blessed One entered the samadhi that expresses the dharma called "profound illumination."

As our story begins, the Buddha enters samadhi, or a state of perfect absorption with no trace of delusion. This particular samadhi expressed the essence of profound illumination. All the lights were on. Everyone was home. Nothing was left out of this luminous state.

And that's kind of the last we hear from the Buddha until the very end of the sutra. Presumably, he wasn't just spacing out. His presence gave rise to the teaching that follows. We all know what it is like to learn something simply by another's presence. It is beyond words. It cuts through discursiveness to convey something beyond words. This, by the way, is one of the twelve methods of teaching the dharma. (Other ways include lecturing or singing, telling amazing stories, and so on.) It's as if everything that happens next is a consequence of that samadhi; if samadhi could talk, this sutra is what it would say.

> ...and at the same time noble Avalokiteshvara,
> the bodhisattva mahasattva, while practicing the
> profound prajnaparamita, saw in this way:
> he saw the five skandhas to be empty of nature.

In many schools of Buddhist thought, there are three figures who represent the qualities of the awakened mind. Manjusri is the bodhisattva of wisdom. Vajrapani is the bodhisattva of power or enlightened activity. Avalokiteshvara is the bodhisattva of compassion. In our story, he is also called the "bodhisattva mahasattva," the greatest of the bodhisattvas. Here, he and the Buddha have a simultaneous realization; the Buddha experiences profound illumination while in samadhi and Avalokitesvara does as well, although by practicing the profound prajnaparamita, the exact text that you and I are also practicing. So it stands to reason that we, too, could see what Avalokitesvara does: that the five skandhas are empty of nature.

Skandhas is usually translated as "heaps." Which doesn't sound all that awesome and, in fact, they are not. They are the source of all our confusion. Although empty of inherent nature, we think they are real. This is where our problems begin.

Much more on the skandhas below. In the meantime, note that realizing their inherent emptiness–meaning that they exist due to causes and conditions rather than having a separate existence–is the same as profound illumination. So hard to understand but so rewarding to try.

> Then, through the power of the Buddha, venerable Shariputra said to noble Avalokiteshvara, the bodhisattva mahasattva, "How should a son or daughter of noble family train, who wishes to practice the profound prajnaparamita?"

Shariputra was also a devoted disciple of the Buddha. He was known for, among other things, great intellect and doctrinal mastery—which make him the perfect person to kick off this conversation about non-duality and the emptiness of all doctrine, most distinctly *not* intellectualization. If Avalokiteshvara can convince him, he can convince anyone. He is, after all, the Bodhisattva Mahasattva: the ultimate bodhisattva. If Shariputra represents wisdom, Avalokiteshvara brings the fullness of compassion. Wisdom and compassion are inseparable, two sides of a single coin. Both are obviously essential, but in this sutra, compassion is the teacher and wisdom the student. One offers and the other receives.

In this sense, both masculine and feminine principles are invoked. Compassion is associated with the masculine and wisdom with the feminine. In Buddhist thought, compassion is not about what you feel but about what you do. Wisdom doesn't refer to what you know but to vast openness beyond concept.

"Son or daughter" is part of the original text. It was not added later for greater inclusivity.

"Noble family" here means practicing Buddhist, but we can think of it as including any and all who seek. AKA you. You are part of the noble family. Like Shariputra, you also want to discover the deepest wisdom, the profound prajnaparamita.

Avalokiteshvara responds to Shariputra's question:

> Addressed in this way, noble Avalokiteshvara, the
> bodhisattva mahasattva, said to venerable Shariputra,
> "O Shariputra, a son or daughter of noble family
> who wishes to practice the profound prajnaparamita
> should see in this way: seeing the five skandhas
> to be empty of nature."

Skandha is a Sanskrit word that means "aggregate" and refers to those parts of us that we think are real, things like our bodies and emotions and so on. It can be quite surprising to learn these things aren't real. I mean, I have a heart. If I cut it, it bleeds. How is it that these things aren't real? Again: I can't answer that in any definitive way. The best I can suggest is to think about it yourself. Also, there is a Buddhist school of thought called *Madhyamika*. Madhyamika practice, associated with the great Tibetan sage Nagarjuna, is also known as the emptiness doctrine. It is a profound examination of what Buddhists call the Middle Way, which refers to spiritual paths that are neither eternalistic (*if I do right, I will end up in a forever-perfect place*) nor nihilistic (*there is no such place, there is only here, now, and me*). The Middle Way is not the midpoint between these two, by the way. Nor is it *not* eternalism or nihilism. Nor is it both. (Yet more confoundment for us).

However, the general point here seems to be what the Heart Sutra is also pointing at: whatever it is, you can't find it, at least not with conventional senses. Even the simple question "who am I?" reveals the utter futility of the search. I mean, you could say *I'm me, I'm Susan, I'm female, I like sandwiches.* Okay then. Where are you located exactly? Are you your brain? Your heart? If you remove a finger, are you still you? How about an arm or a pancreas? Are "you" located in any of these places? This is like a Buddhist rendition of the Abbott and Costello bit, *Who's on First?* Try to prove that any of the skandhas are real. Email me with proof, please! But first watch *Who's on First.*

Our true being goes far beyond form (physicality), feeling, perception, formation (our judgments, conclusions, opinions), and consciousness—the five skandhas. Actually, says Avalokiteshvara, while those things appear to be solid, they are empty.

Emptiness is a core concept in the Buddhadharma. If I could explain it, this would be the place to do so. Unfortunately, I cannot. I have spent decades looking for the true meaning of emptiness, only to come up…empty handed. Perhaps this is closer to the truth than any point-by-point academic view. What I can deduce is that emptiness does not mean null and void. It doesn't mean non-existent. (It would be horrific to discover that at the core of Buddhist teachings is the revelation that everything is dead.) Rather, emptiness means empty of separate existence. You didn't get here in a space capsule, presumably. You are made of your parents. Their parents. The environment everyone grew up in. The sandwiches they ate. The notions they passed down. You are made up of all of this and if a single contributing factor was deleted, you wouldn't be here. You're empty of separate existence. But here you are. Empty and luminous. This seems to be the direction the Heart Sutra points us in—all phenomena are empty. And luminous. And empty. And luminous. In this way, emptiness might just as well be called fullness. There is nothing that is not separate from you. Conversely, you are not separate from anything.

(Once I heard a story from a Tibetan Lama. He was studying in his office and on the bookshelves behind him were countless volumes of a single text. A student entered and asked what all those volumes said. "They say you're not here," he answered.)

Back to our program: Avalokiteshvara says everything you think is you: your form, feelings, perceptions, formations, and even your consciousness are empty. He's not saying they aren't here, by the way. Just that they aren't what you think they are.

This misunderstanding is the beginning of human suffering because it marks the beginning of wrong view.

He continues:

"Form is emptiness; emptiness also is form. Emptiness is no other than form; form is no other than emptiness. In the same way, feeling, perception, formation, and consciousness are emptiness. Thus, Shariputra, all dharmas are emptiness. There are no characteristics. There is no birth and no cessation. There is no impurity and no purity. There is no decrease and no increase."

———

The first skandha, form, is not just empty—it is emptiness. He continues: *Emptiness is no other than form*...etc. So it's not just that all forms are empty. Emptiness is also a form and therefore empty of...itself? Your guess is as good as mine. And let's not stop with the first skandha, form. The others are empty too. By this logic, you could say feeling is emptiness, emptiness also is feeling. Perception is emptiness, emptiness also is perception. Thanks a lot, Buddha.

This turns out to be our next instruction: all dharmas (teachings) are emptiness. Everything you have ever studied or thought you grasped, poof, empty.

This was big news to the monastics present. They had devoted their lives to mastering the teachings and were now told those teachings didn't even exist. According to the lore, this was too much to bear and some of the monastics simply expired. (One of my favorite books about the Heart Sutra is called *The Heart Attack Sutra*.)

> "Therefore, Shariputra, in emptiness, there is no form, no feeling, no perception, no formation, no consciousness; no eye, no ear, no nose, no tongue, no body, no mind; no appearance, no sound, no smell, no taste, no touch, no dharmas; no eye dhatu up to no mind dhatu, no dhatu of dharmas, no mind consciousness dhatu…"

Avalokiteshvara repeats "no" to the five skandhas and then adds in what arises from each skandha. Each skandha then gives rise to a sense perception. The skandha of form gives rise to the eye. The skandha of feeling gives rise to our ears. Perception is associated with the sense perception of smell, formation with taste, and consciousness with touch. Further, each sense perception has its own discrete consciousness or *dhatu*. There is eye-consciousness, ear-consciousness, and so on, up to mind-consciousness. The sutra chooses not to elucidate each dhatu but instead says "no eye dhatu up to no mind dhatu."

The skandhas, sense perceptions, and dhatus are what create suffering. One could reasonably think, *if I just realize the insubstantiality of skandhas up to dhatus, I won't suffer. I'd be fully in the know.* If only. Then Avalokiteshvara goes on to say there is ignorance and also no end of ignorance, so forget about being in the know or not. Both are insubstantial. While he's at it, he throws in birth, old age, sickness, and death as things that don't exist and don't *not* exist. So if you were hoping to become enlightened in order to transcend birth, old age, sickness, and death (i.e. samsara), you're out of luck. You're also completely in luck since they don't exist to begin with.

> "...no ignorance, no end of ignorance up to no old age and death, no end of old age and death..."

Samsaric suffering begins with ignorance or an incorrect view of reality. A view that the Heart Sutra rights by presenting the awakened aspect of ignorance: wisdom. Suffering begins with ignorance and concludes with birth, old age, sickness, and death. In between are mental formations (ideas, opinions), dualistic consciousness, name and form (the labels we give to forms like "chair" or "winter" or "blueberry"), the six senses (mentioned already), contact (that which connects what you sense with what you call it), feeling or sensation, craving, grasping, becoming (or reifying), concluding with our old friends, birth, and old age and death. This list comprises the 12 nidanas (Pali, meaning source) depicted in Wheels of Life paintings and other Buddhist iconography. Avalokiteshvara is not saying those things don't exist. He's saying they do and they don't. Alrighty then.

"...no suffering, no origin of suffering, no cessation of suffering, no path, no wisdom, no attainment, and no nonattainment."

―

To conclude, he obliterates the most central teachings of Buddhism: the Four Noble Truths. (I wonder how the author of these truths, the Buddha himself, felt about hearing this. Fine, apparently. See: conclusion of sutra.)

The Four Noble Truths are:
1. Life is suffering
2. The cause of suffering (grasping)
3. The cessation of suffering (stop grasping)
4. The path out of suffering (the Noble Eightfold Path)

When Avalokiteshvara says "no suffering, no origin of suffering, no cessation of suffering, no path" he knocks out each noble truth, one by one. There is no such thing as wisdom. Nothing to attain. Nothing to not attain. No wonder some folks fainted or worse.

> "Therefore, Shariputra, since the bodhisattvas have no attainment, they abide by means of prajnaparamita. Since there is no obscuration of mind, there is no fear. They transcend falsity and attain complete nirvana."

As mentioned, bodhisattvas are those practitioners who seek enlightenment in order to be of benefit to others—enlightenment being the way one transcends all suffering, including birth, old age, sickness, and death. Enlightened beings peace out to… somewhere. I don't really know where, perhaps to higher realms or some other great place. However, enlightened bodhisattvas do not peace out. Part of their vow is to continue to return to this earthly realm in whatever form may be of most benefit until all beings are enlightened. And by "all," the vow means ALL. Human beings, animal beings, insects, birds, and, perhaps, life forms we can't yet see. So, ALL. Apparently, for bodhisattvas, this is no problem. They live within or, one could say, *are* ultimate wisdom.

Then, my very favorite line which says they completely transcend falsity. Doing so eradicates fear altogether. They're not worried about what might happen if they come back in a future life as a bug or a kitty cat or the president of the United States. It's literally all good because in each case there is 0 percent departure from the inseparability of samsara and nirvana.

Inexplicable Joy

> "All the buddhas of the three times, by means of prajnaparamita, fully awaken to unsurpassable, true, complete enlightenment."

In Buddhist cosmology, there have been and will be many Buddhas. In our reality, Siddhartha Guatama was our Buddha. There have been other Buddhas in the past, there are some in the present, and there will be more in the future. Past, present, and future are the "three times." No matter where they appear in the space-time continuum, all are fully awake. They got that way through the wisdom that transcends all boundaries, all space, all time, all continua.

"Therefore, the great mantra of prajnaparamita, the mantra of great insight, the unsurpassed mantra, the unequaled mantra, the mantra that calms all suffering, should be known as truth, since there is no deception. The prajnaparamita mantra is said in this way: OM GATE GATE PARAGATE PARASAMGATE BODHI SVAHA"

―――

A mantra is a mind training tool that supports your mind to be used for something other than thinking about how great or how awful you are, all the things you have to do, what you really think about this person or that. I'm not saying such thoughts are useless. You have to be very practical and attuned to the details of your life and this world. However, when these are the only things you use your mind for, you remain tethered to the realm of suffering. Even thinking about how to make the world a better place keeps us in the realm of duality.

Many people think that the solution to all of this is simply to stop thinking…anything. "Clear the mind of thought" is often an instruction given in meditation practice. Oh please. It so happens that our minds do not have an off switch. Thinking you should stop thinking is itself a thought. We are bound for Palookaville.

In my Buddhist tradition (Vajrayana or Tibetan Buddhism), the mind is considered a sense perception. The Heart Sutra itself reinforces this by placing on equal footing "eye, ear, nose, tongue" with mind. If the mind is a sense perception, then, it simply produces thought as part of its job just as the eyes see and the ears hear. And, like eyes, ears, and so on, there is no off switch. Just as you can't open your eyes and not see anything (although you are invited to try), you can't have a mind and then will yourself not to think anything. It doesn't seem to quiet down by grit and determination. Rather, as we relax, the activity of our mind changes on its own, just as our vision may start to shimmer when we soften our gaze.

Relaxing is also not achieved by will or internal exhortations to shut up. However, mantra can accomplish some of what we seek by replacing discursive thoughts with profound syllables that don't mean anything and, at the same time, mean everything. Everything beyond words, that is.

Each syllable of a mantra invokes a particular power or quality. Just as music is beyond words but conveys something very particular, so do mantras. For example, OM MANI PADME HUM means, very loosely: Enlightenment (OM); Jewel (MANI), associated here with wisdom; Lotus (PADME), associated with compassion; Inseparable (HUM). When you chant OM MANI PADME HUM, you are saying *Enlightenment, Wisdom, Compassion, Inseparable*...but without thinking those things.

Often, in Vajrayana Buddhist practices, mantras accompany certain visualizations. For example, one might chant (audibly or silently) OM AH HUM VAJRA GURU PADMA SIDHHI HUM while visualizing the great sage Padmasambhava, also known as Guru Rinpoche or the Second Buddha. (Padmasambhava and his collaborator, Yeshe Tsogyal, brought Buddhism to Tibet so Tibetan practices tend to really appreciate them.) Practices associated with Guru Rinpoche and Yeshe Tsogyal have been central to my personal practice for more than a decade. I have been given teachings on visualizations (which means imagining or experiencing rather than literal seeing) and mantras meant to invoke them. However, try as I might—and I have tried for weeks, months, years—I remained terrible at visualizing. At one point, I just said enough is enough and instead of visualizing this very complex image in my mind's eye, I suggested to myself that I just hear the mantra. In my mind's ear? This came much easier. When I told my meditation teacher about this, he said—humblebrag coming up—"smart woman." I took this to mean that A) it was fine to do this and B) mantras contain the full meaning, just as full as the most detailed image.

So, if you've ever thought "I wonder if there is a mantra that calms all suffering," the answer is yes: OM GATE GATE PARAGATE PARASAMGATE BODHI SVAHA. The Heart Sutra then goes on to offer the ultimate mantra; great, deep, unsurpassed, and (pay very close attention here) *calms all suffering.*

OM means many things including, as mentioned, enlightenment. So with the first syllable, we know what we're talking about here. Full liberation.

GATE (pronounced *gah-tay*) means "gone beyond." *Gate* is then repeated in case you missed it the first time.

PARAGATE means really gone beyond.

PARASAMGATE means really, *really* gone beyond. Fully. Totally. Absolutely beyond all duality, even beyond going beyond.

BODHI means awake (same root as the words Buddha and bodhisattva).

SVAHA means something like Hallelujah! Hail! Yay!

So the prajnaparamita mantra is something like "Enlightenment, gone beyond, really gone beyond, totally gone beyond, AWAKE, mic drop." (This is my translation.)

"Thus, Shariputra, the bodhisattva mahasattva should train in the profound prajnaparamita."

―――

So, says Avalokiteshvara, please pick up what I'm putting down. This concludes my remarks.

> Then the Blessed One arose from that samadhi and praised noble Avalokiteshvara, the bodhisattva mahasattva, saying, "Good, good, O son of noble family; thus it is, O son of noble family, thus it is. One should practice the profound prajnaparamita just as you have taught and all the tathagatas will rejoice."

All this time, the Buddha was resting in the samadhi of profound illumination, embodying in human form the truth of what Avalokiteshvara taught. He fully signed off on Avalokiteshvara's answer and indicated that all the *tathagatas* (other Buddhas, presumably of the three times) would be equally delighted.

When the Blessed One had said this, venerable Shariputra and noble Avalokiteshvara, the bodhisattva mahasattva, that whole assembly and the world with its gods, humans, asuras, and gandharvas rejoiced and praised the words of the Blessed One.

―――

Once the Buddha signed off on Avalokiteshvara's answer to Shariputra's question, everyone was content, including Shariputra and noble Avalokiteshvara. Additionally, gods, humans, asuras, and gandharvas were pleased.

In Buddhist cosmology, there are six realms of existence (though not all are mentioned in the text). Some say that the realms illustrate six psychological states while others say they are completely real, literal. You will have to make up your own mind.

Until we become fully enlightened, we are bound to take rebirth in one realm or another. The human realm (where we are) is just one of them. It is the most advantageous realm of all as we have the right ratio of suffering to ease. We are able to reflect, learn, and perceive. Though extremely difficult to accomplish, we in the human realm stand the best chance of becoming enlightened.

The god realm is a place of great pleasure and ease. Beings who dwell there can fly, receive accurate psychic data, flow from one moment to the next with satisfaction and delight. It sounds pretty damn good if you ask me; however, it is still a place of samsaric suffering. Though life spans are healthy and long (like, Methusaleh long), death is extremely painful and drawn out.

Everything else may go their way, but god realm beings are unlikely to attain enlightenment and transcend the realms of being. There is not enough pain to propel one onto the spiritual path, so rebirth will take place and the cycling of suffering will begin again. Each realm is said to have a different Buddha on call. In the god realm, all this particular Buddha can do is play a musical instrument. There is no point in teaching those who have no problems.

If you've ever had a day (or a moment) when you felt thoroughly at ease, cocooned in pleasure, unworried, with no immediate possibility of hassle, you have touched in with the feelings of the gods.

Asuras inhabit the jealous god realm. Like gods, they are also considered fortunate but they are not satisfied with what they have. They want more. They suffer from jealousy. *That god over there seems to have more than me, I need to take it for myself* is a common state of mind. Wars are waged and much effort is invested in protecting and increasing one's domain. It is easy to understand this mindset when, say, scrolling through any social media account. It seems that we all turn into asuras when confronted with perfect people living perfect lives, or even expressing flaws in a way that indicates their flawless mindfulness. Tech CEOs, bitter politicians, and craven spiritual influencers abound.

Though the Buddha does not name them, there are three more realms. In the Hungry Ghost realm, live beings with tiny mouths, narrow throats, and huge bellies. They are always hungry but can never be filled to satisfaction. I think we all know what this feels like. The animal realm includes actual animals and also refers to that state where we fall into a stupor created and reinforced by a favored narcotic: gaming, doom-scrolling, addictive television watching, and actual narcotics are included, as is anything else we do to distract ourselves from reality. Even noble pursuits such as academic study and deep self-reflection, when undertaken reflexively, are prone to animal realm-like qualities. Then there is the hell realm, an actual place of torment and suffering beyond words. In Buddhist cosmology, there are many hells: hot hells, cold hells, and so on. (For an overview of the hell realms, please refer to this astonishing work, *A Guided Tour of Hell,* by my own meditation teacher, Samuel Bercholz.)

Finally, the Buddha mentions *gandharvas*, celestial beings associated with music and dance. They don't eat food but are nourished instead by scent. I wish I knew more about them. I think of them (correctly or not) as dream-like accompanists who find us between realms: birth and death, wakefulness and sleep, spaced out or awake. Whoever they are, they, too, were extremely pleased by the words of the Blessed One.

Parenthetically, the source of happiness for all these beings, including the tathagatas (those who have gone beyond, aka Buddhas), seemed to be the Buddha's praise of Avalokiteshvara rather than Avalokiteshvara's extraordinary explication.

So...was Shariputra's initiating question—*How should a son or daughter of noble family train who wishes to practice the profound prajnaparamita*—answered?

Now you have to figure it out.

ON CHANTING

A while ago, I was on Zoom with a group of teachers to plan for an upcoming 10-day Heart Sutra retreat I was leading in Colorado. We were a group of six: five women and one man. The man was my co-teacher and I was really happy about this because we knew each other well and I had enormous love and respect for him. I had supported him on the last retreat we co-taught and this time, I was the lead teacher and so I conducted the meeting. As we concluded, he said, "it's really interesting to see how this retreat is coming together—quite different from when I was the lead teacher." This was not meant as praise or critique. We had both agreed that our previous experience working together was wonderful. Rather, his comment was about seeing the difference between the way feminine and masculine principles (which have nothing to do with gender, as always bears repeating) create an experience. When feminine principle was activated, we discovered the retreat rather than mandated it. We felt into it together. We raised it as one might raise a revival tent.

To practice the Heart Sutra, this is a good approach. Rather than limiting oneself to discovering the meaning word by word, we co-rouse the meaning together. As with any great work of writing, it begins to pervade the atmosphere. We see it in our surroundings. We hear it in others' voices. We find that it has set up camp in our minds and dances with habitual thought patterns to create new rhythms. When this happens with a book, there can be a sense of heartbreak when it's over. *I will miss you, my friend. I enjoyed cohabitating with you. I hope to see you again...*

Luckily, the Heart Sutra is never over, and you can live together every day of your life. This daily communion is known as spiritual practice. As with all long-term relationships, at some point the power no longer comes from joyful discovery but from the longevity itself.

This is a style of learning consonant with the feminine principle. According to this principle, learning happens along three concurrent lines.

We pay attention to the words, the *sound* of the words, and the environment within which the words are spoken.

A great way to experiment with this is by listening to music. The meaning comes through via the particular words and notes, the sound of the words and notes, and, somehow, the environment feels altered by the presence of the music. Right now, you could take a moment and listen to "Dedicated to You" from John Coltrane and Johnny Hartman. (Always a good recommendation, if you ask me.) Listen first to the meaning of the words. Listen again to the sound of the words; let their meaning fall to the background. Listen a third time while looking around wherever it is that you are—your bedroom, the bus, a park bench. See how the world changes as you listen. Stay where you are and now try this exercise again with "Jump Around" from House of Pain. Listen to the meaning. The sound. The environment. I just happened to pick two tracks that I have listened to countless times but of course you can choose any songs you like. The meaning will continue to show itself along three lines.

Traditionally, the Heart Sutra is chanted in a flowing monotone. The idea is to let the words flow like a river, no phrasing, no stopping at the end of sentences; just keep going.

The suggested time to chant the Heart Sutra is just before your meditation practice, although you can chant it any time you like. It traditionally happens in a rhythm, metronomically. Not too slow, not too fast—steadily, continuously. Often people wonder why it is vocalized this way. Please try it and then ask yourself why. Say every single word, including the title (which begins a bit more slowly) and at the end of the first phrase, *Once the Blessed One was dwelling...* establish the pace you will stick to for the remainder of the chant, up until the last phrase. *On... the words of the Blessed One*, slow down again so that *one* comes out like an exhale.

IN CONCLUSION

Recently, as mentioned, I was set to teach a 10-day Heart Sutra program at a remote retreat center in the Colorado Rockies. I arrived a few days early to acclimate to the altitude and prepare for what, to me, was an extremely important undertaking. Teaching the Heart Sutra is not an academic exercise. It has more to do with transmitting something rather than explaining it. I wanted my mind to be settled and open.

While there, I saw another retreat was just wrapping up. Renowned artist Kazuaki Tanahashi Sensei was leading a calligraphy program. It so happens that this 94-year old teacher had also written a truly profound book on the Heart Sutra, subtitled *A Comprehensive Guide to the Classic of Mahayana Buddhism*. And comprehensive it is, full of historic and dharmic references based on his *70+ years* of practice and study.

Suddenly, I was semi-embarrassed. How could I teach on this topic when a genuine master was present? Each time I passed him on the way to the dining tent or program hall, I waited until he went by to make a slight bow of respect, outside of his field of vision. I didn't want to call attention to myself or make him feel he needed to acknowledge me back. A few days went by like this, with me hoping to osmotically absorb some of his wisdom while furtively bowing into the space behind him.

On the day his program ended, I walked into the residential lodge and saw him sitting in the vestibule by himself with his suitcase, waiting, presumably, to be picked up and transported to his next destination. This time I bowed to him directly and exited the vestibule without stopping or speaking. With three steps into the main building, I thought, *don't let this moment pass.* I went back in and told him I was leading a Heart Sutra retreat, would he mind if I asked him a question. He nodded assent. "If you could tell students one thing about this text, what would it be?" Without missing a beat, he replied, "Most important is the final word of the mantra: *svaha.*" Svaha! He continued, "It is most often translated as 'so be it' but it can also mean joy."

I had never heard this before. I thought of svaha as something like *mic drop* (as mentioned). We said a few more things I cannot recall, probably me bumbling around trying to appreciate him while also leaving him to himself as quickly as possible. (What do I know about human interactions?)

I thought through this reinterpretation of *Om gate, gate, paragate, parasamgate, bodhi, svaha* and tried to imagine how the entire text could be reconsidered if *Om, gone, gone, gone beyond, truly gone beyond, awake, so be it* also meant *Om, gone, gone, gone beyond, truly gone beyond, awake, joy*!

All I could think at the time was, *He's just given me the seed syllable for the upcoming retreat. Focus on joy. See what happens.* And so I did. Whether the seed blossomed due to circumstance or secret arrangements made by powers beyond my ken (perhaps these are no different?), joy was present. Amidst the uncertainty about the meaning of the text, physical discomforts that come with sitting long hours, the other-worldly sound of chanting in a monotone, altitude-related somatic weirdness, worries about COVID (well-founded, as it turned out; the retreat closed a few days early), the overriding feeling was of joy. Everyday, a new rainbow. Actual ravens cawing during a particular protector chant that mentioned "the raven-headed one." Community. Love. Insight. But this was a strange kind of joy. Happy, yes, but also sad. Full. Objectless. Present in laughter and even more so in tears. What is this strange joy?

Then I read this:

Deep sadness, because nothing lasts.
Fervent love, because all beings are my beloved family.
Lucid openness, because this ordinary mind is full awakening.
Sheer joy, because all of this is true.
—CHOKYI NYIMA RINPOCHE from *Sadness, Love, Openness*

May the Heart Sutra perfume your world with this inexplicable joy.

RESOURCES

The Sutra of the Heart of Transcendent Knowledge
(Commentary)
NALANDA TRANSLATION COMMITTEE

The Heart Attack Sutra
KARL BRUNNHOLZL

The Heart Sutra
KAZUAKI TANAHASHI

The Heart of Unconditional Love
TULKU THONDUP RINPOCHE

ACKNOWLEDGMENTS

All thanks go to my dearest heart friend and cosmic seer into my particular journey, Sam Bercholz. You knew me before we ever met. Thank you for introducing me to the Heart Sutra, the seed syllable for my entire journey.

Inexpressible gratitude to my dharma sister, Crystal Gandrud, for editing and encouraging (and understanding) this work from your home on the genius planet.

Thank you to Leanna Kristine for her careful and insightful copy edit of this material. In addition, she and Geneviève Okuma kept the Open Heart Project steady and loving while I worked on this book.

Thank you to everyone in the Open Heart Project sangha. You are a constant source of inspiration. I wrote this book for you.

And to Tulku Thondop Rinpoche, a living emanation of AH.

ABOUT THE AUTHOR

Susan Piver is the *New York Times* bestselling author of many books, including *The Hard Questions*; the award-winning *How Not to Be Afraid of Your Own Life*; *The Wisdom of a Broken Heart*; *Start Here Now: An Open-Hearted Guide to the Path and Practice of Meditation*; *The Four Noble Truths of Love: Buddhist Wisdom for Modern Relationships*, and *The Buddhist Enneagram: Nine Paths to Warriorship*.

Susan has an international reputation as a skillful meditation teacher. She has given talks everywhere, including Procter & Gamble, Google Paris, Google London, and Harvard University.

A student of Buddhism since 1993, Susan graduated from a Buddhist seminary in 2004. In 2012, she founded The Open Heart Project, the world's largest online-only dharma center. The Open Heart Project offers meditation classes, virtual retreats, and community gatherings. In 2018, she and Crystal Gandrud created a publishing imprint, Lionheart Press, to offer books that merge Buddhism with everyday life.

ABOUT THE OPEN HEART PROJECT

The Open Heart Project is a unique online gathering space for people who want to go deeply into wisdom traditions, but without signing up for someone else's ideas about how their reality should work. All the courses, workshops, retreats, meditations, gatherings, and publications created by the OHP are offered as a way to circumvent dharma-splaining about what is most intimate and precious—your own heart and mind. Everything we do is designed to compel you to go more deeply into your own wisdom with the support of very traditional Buddhist teachings.

This short work on the Heart Sutra is intended in exactly this way. It presents very traditional teachings but in a very ordinary voice, including personal stories to illustrate the pith. As with this book, we don't want to pretend we know more than you—just that we have been doing it for longer and so share from a place of greater experience.

Please visit openheartproject.com for more.

OTHER BOOKS FROM LIONHEART PRESS

Founded by Susan Piver and Crystal Gandrud, Lionheart Press offers books that merge Buddhism with everyday life. Wherever it takes hold, Buddhist wisdom transforms its environment, but Buddhism is also changed by its environment. That is the magical, resilient alchemy of truth. Nothing static, nothing stale.

LIONHEARTPRESS.NET

BY SUSAN PIVER
The Four Noble Truths of Love: Buddhist Wisdom for Modern Relationships
The Buddhist Enneagram: Nine Paths to Warriorship

BY JENNA HOLLENSTEIN
Eat to Love: A Mindful Guide to Transforming Your Relationship with Food, Body, and Life
Mommysattva: Contemplations for Mothers who Meditate

BY KEVIN TOWNLEY
Look, Look, Look, Look, Look Again: Buddhist Wisdom Reflected in 26 Artists

www.ingramcontent.com/pod-product-compliance
Lightning Source LLC
Chambersburg PA
CBHW060621080526
44585CB00013B/930